This edition first published in 2023 by Bellwether Media, Inc.

No part of this publication may be reproduced in whole or in part without written permission of the publisher. For information regarding permission, write to Bellwether Media, Inc., Attention: Permissions Department, 6012 Blue Circle Drive, Minnetonka, MN 55343.

Library of Congress Cataloging-in-Publication Data

Names: Morey, Allan, author.
Title: Patrick Mahomes / by Allan Morey.
Description: Minneapolis, MN : Bellwether Media, 2023. | Series: Torque. Sport's superstars | Includes bibliographical references and index. | Audience: Ages 7-12 | Audience: Grades 4-6 | Summary: "Engaging images accompany information about Patrick Mahomes. The combination of high-interest subject matter and light text is intended for students in grades 3 through 7"– Provided by publisher.
Identifiers: LCCN 2022050065 (print) | LCCN 2022050066 (ebook) | ISBN 9798887871593 (library binding) | ISBN 9798887872859 (ebook)
Subjects: LCSH: Mahomes, Patrick, 1995– –Juvenile literature. | Quarterbacks (Football)–United States–Biography–Juvenile literature.
Classification: LCC GV939.M284 M67 2023 (print) | LCC GV939.M284 (ebook) | DDC 796.332092 [B]–dc23/eng/20221019
LC record available at https://lccn.loc.gov/2022050065
LC ebook record available at https://lccn.loc.gov/2022050066

Text copyright © 2023 by Bellwether Media, Inc. TORQUE and associated logos are trademarks and/or registered trademarks of Bellwether Media, Inc.

Editor: Rebecca Sabelko   Designer: Gabriel Hilger

Printed in the United States of America, North Mankato, MN.

Torque brims with excitement perfect for thrill-seekers of all kinds. Discover daring survival skills, explore uncharted worlds, and marvel at mighty engines and extreme sports. In *Torque* books, anything can happen. Are you ready?

TABLE OF CONTENTS

- TOUCHDOWN FOR MAHOMES! 4
- WHO IS PATRICK MAHOMES? 6
- GETTING INTO THE GAME 8
- A SUPERSTAR 12
- LOOKING INTO THE FUTURE 20
- GLOSSARY 22
- TO LEARN MORE 23
- INDEX 24

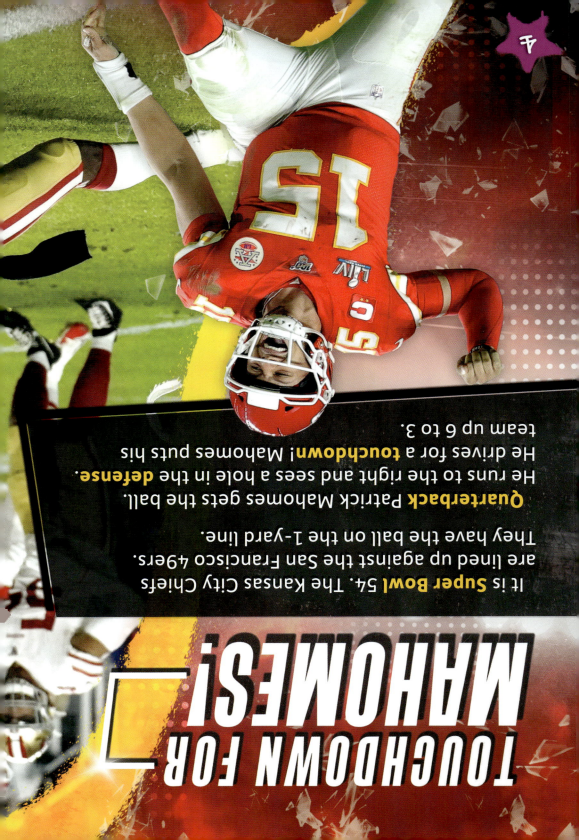

TOUCHDOWN FOR MAHOMES!

It is **Super Bowl 54**. The Kansas City Chiefs are lined up against the San Francisco 49ers. They have the ball on the 1-yard line. **Quarterback** Patrick Mahomes gets the ball. He runs to the right and sees a hole in the **defense**. He drives for a **touchdown!** Mahomes puts his team up 6 to 3.

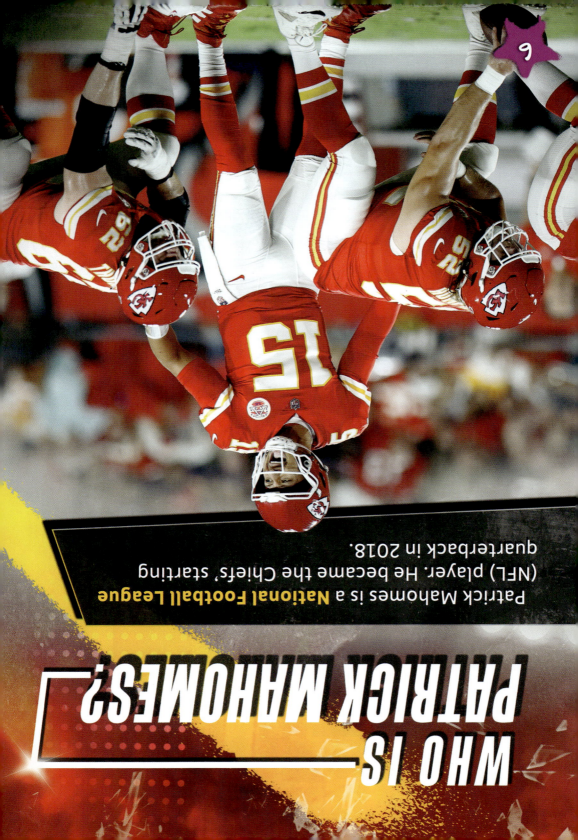

WHO IS PATRICK MAHOMES?

Patrick Mahomes is a **National Football League** (NFL) player. He became the Chiefs' starting quarterback in 2018.

7

Mahomes is known for throwing touchdowns. He has thrown more than 150! But he is also known for running the ball. Mahomes has run for more than 1,200 yards.

PATRICK MAHOMES

BIRTHDAY	September 17, 1995
HOMETOWN	Tyler, Texas
POSITION	quarterback
HEIGHT	6 feet 3 inches
DRAFTED	Kansas City Chiefs in the 1st round (10th overall) of the 2017 NFL Draft

GETTING INTO THE GAME

Mahomes grew up playing several sports. He was a baseball and basketball star in high school.

Mahomes also tried out for football. He spent much of his time on defense. But he hoped to play quarterback. Soon, he proved his skills. Many coaches took notice.

MLB DRAFT

IN 2014, THE DETROIT TIGERS DRAFTED MAHOMES IN THE 37TH ROUND OF THE BASEBALL DRAFT. HE CHOSE TO GO TO COLLEGE INSTEAD OF BECOMING A BASEBALL PLAYER.

FAVORITES

HOBBY: golfing
FOOD: ketchup
MOVIE: Remember the Titans
BASEBALL PLAYER: Alex Rodriguez

After high school, Mahomes played football for the Texas Tech Red Raiders. He became a better quarterback and learned how to run the ball. During his second year, Mahomes threw 36 touchdowns and ran for 10.

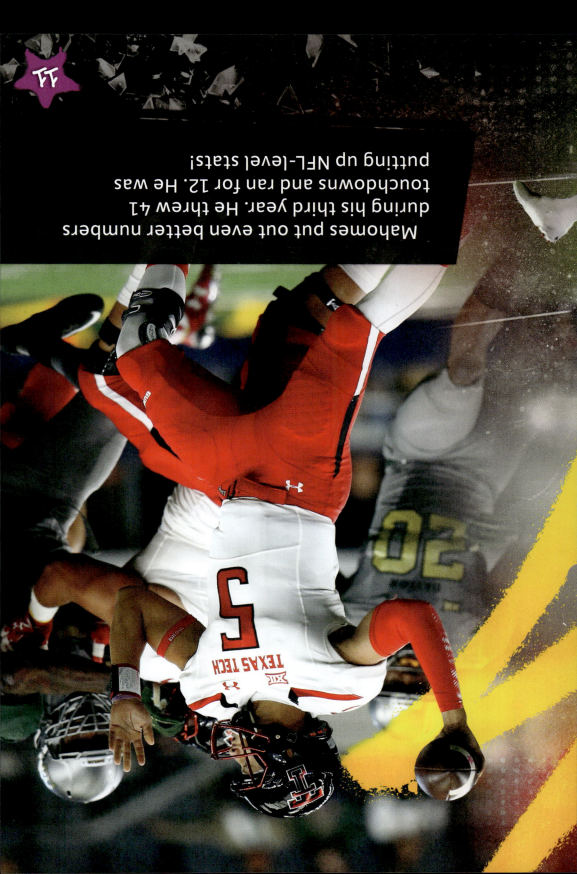

Mahomes put out even better numbers during his third year. He threw 41 touchdowns and ran for 12. He was putting up NFL-level stats!

A SUPERSTAR

In 2017, Mahomes decided to skip his fourth year of college. He entered the NFL **Draft**. The Kansas City Chiefs picked him in the first round. Mahomes spent his **rookie** season as a backup quarterback to Alex Smith. But Smith went to another team in 2018. Mahomes became the leader of the Chiefs!

2017 NFL DRAFT

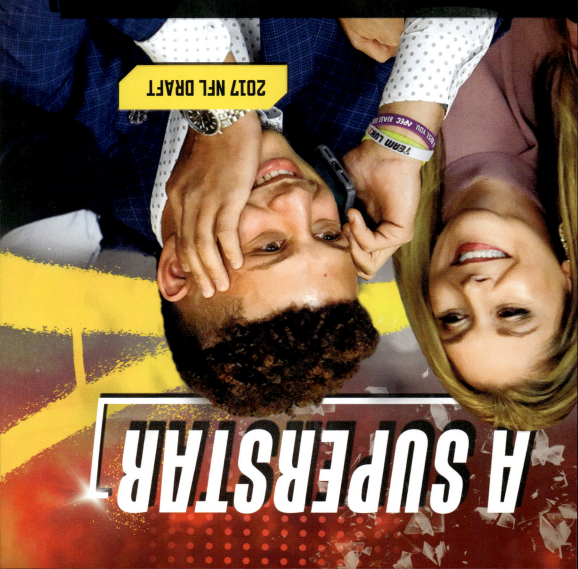

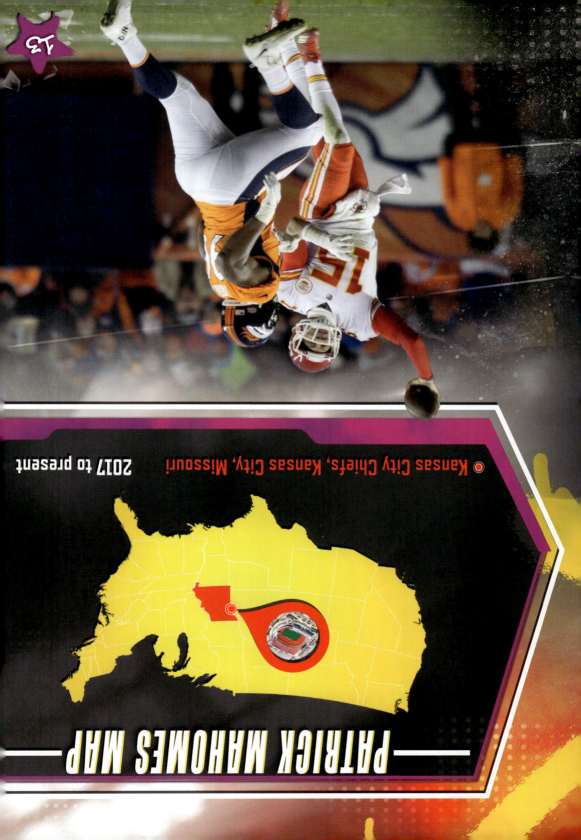

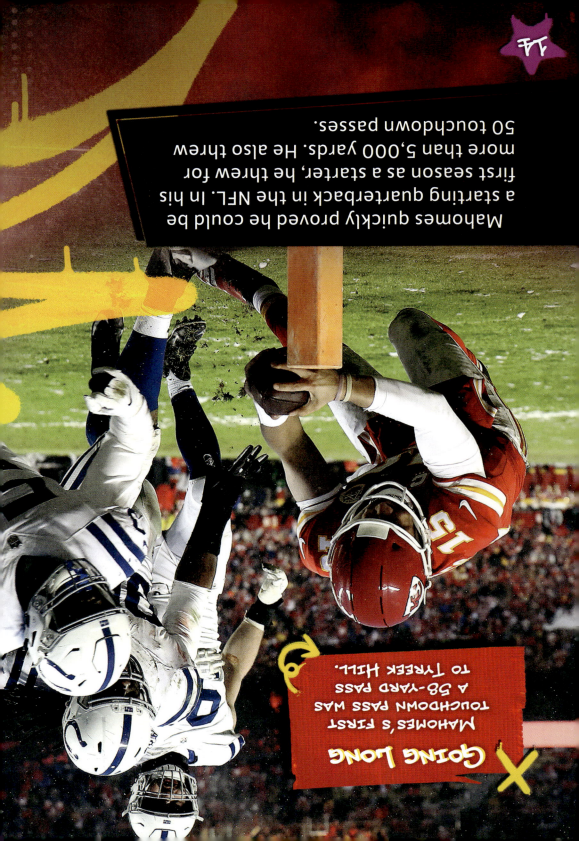

Mahomes quickly proved he could be a starting quarterback in the NFL. In his first season as a starter, he threw for more than 5,000 yards. He also threw 50 touchdown passes.

Going Long

Mahomes's first touchdown pass was a 58-yard pass to Tyreek Hill.

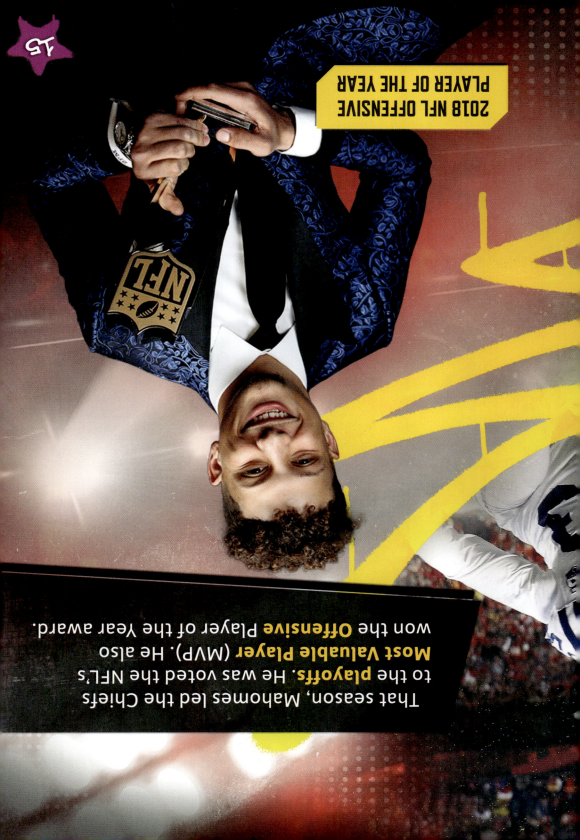

2018 NFL OFFENSIVE PLAYER OF THE YEAR

That season, Mahomes led the Chiefs to the **playoffs**. He was voted the NFL's **Most Valuable Player (MVP)**. He also won the **Offensive** Player of the Year award.

Mahomes had a strong start to the 2019–2020 season. But during a game against the Denver Broncos, Mahomes injured his knee. Luckily, he only missed two games.

That season, Mahomes led the Chiefs back to the playoffs. They won Super Bowl 54 against the 49ers. Mahomes was voted the game's MVP!

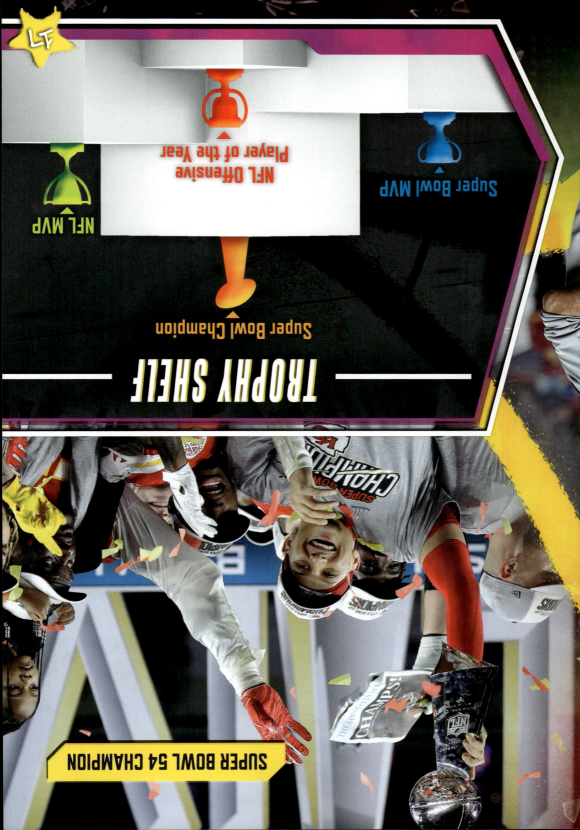

TIMELINE

— 2017 —

The Chiefs pick Mahomes in the first round of the NFL draft

— 2018 —

Mahomes becomes the starting quarterback for the Chiefs

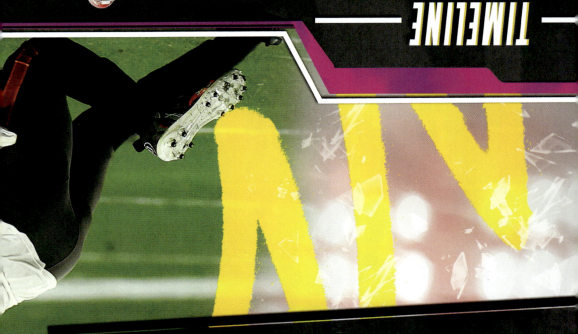

In the 2020–2021 season, Mahomes once again led the Chiefs to the Super Bowl. But they lost to the Tampa Bay Buccaneers 31 to 9. Mahomes led the Chiefs to the playoffs for the fourth time in a row during the 2021–2022 season. But they did not reach the Super Bowl.

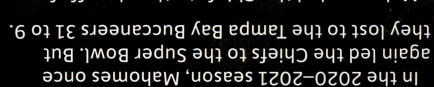

— 2021–2022 —
Mahomes leads the Chiefs to the playoffs for the fourth time in a row

— 2020 —
Mahomes and the Chiefs win Super Bowl 54

— 2018 —
Mahomes is the NFL MVP and Offensive Player of the Year

LOOKING INTO THE FUTURE

In 2019, Mahomes founded 15 and the Mahomies. It supports many youth programs. It hopes to improve the lives of kids!

BACK TO HIS ROOTS

Baseball was the first sport Mahomes was interested in playing. Now he is part-owner of the Kansas City Royals baseball team.

20

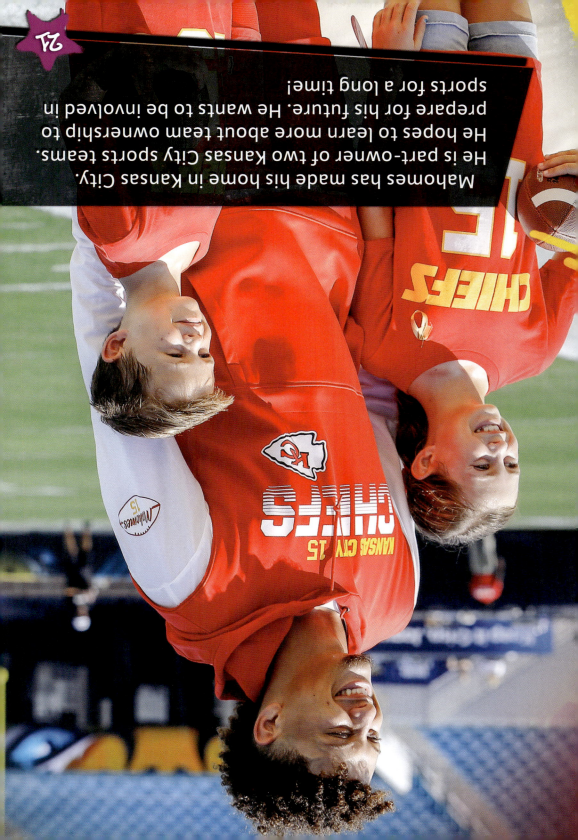

Mahomes has made his home in Kansas City. He is part-owner of two Kansas City sports teams. He hopes to learn more about team ownership to prepare for his future. He wants to be involved in sports for a long time!

GLOSSARY

defense—a group of players who try to stop the opposing team from scoring

draft—a process during which professional teams choose high school and college players to play for them

most valuable player—the best player in a year, game, or series; the most valuable player is often called the MVP.

National Football League—a professional football league in the United States; the National Football League is often called the NFL.

offensive—related to players who have the ball and are trying to score

playoffs—games played after the regular season is over; playoff games determine which teams play in the Super Bowl.

quarterback—a player on offense whose main job is to throw and hand off the ball

rookie—related to a first-year player in a sports league

Super Bowl—the annual championship game of the National Football League

touchdown—a score that occurs when a team crosses into their opponent's end zone with the football; a touchdown is worth six points.

TO LEARN MORE!

AT THE LIBRARY

Grack, Rachel. *Missouri.* Minneapolis, Minn.: Bellwether Media, 2022.

Levit, Joe. *Meet Patrick Mahomes.* Minneapolis, Minn.: Lerner Publications, 2023.

Rustad, Martha E. H. *What You Never Knew about Patrick Mahomes.* North Mankato, Minn.: Capstone, 2022.

ON THE WEB

Factsurfer.com gives you a safe, fun way to find more information.

1. Go to www.factsurfer.com
2. Enter "Patrick Mahomes" into the search box and click 🔍.
3. Select your book cover to see a list of related content.

INDEX

15 and the Mahomies, 20
awards, 15, 16, 17
baseball, 8, 9, 20
basketball, 8
childhood, 8
draft, 9, 12
favorites, 9
future, 20, 21
injury, 16
Kansas City Chiefs, 4, 5, 6, 12, 15, 16, 18
map, 13
Most Valuable Player, 15, 16
National Football League, 6, 11, 12, 14, 15
playoffs, 15, 16, 18
profile, 7
quarterback, 4, 6, 8, 10, 12, 14
rookie, 12
Super Bowl, 4, 5, 16, 17, 18
Texas Tech Red Raiders, 10
timeline, 18–19
touchdown, 4, 7, 10, 11, 14
trophy shelf, 17

The images in this book are reproduced through the courtesy of: Focus On Sport/ Contributor/ Getty Images, front cover; David Eulitt/ Contributor/ Getty Images, p. 3; Maddie Meyer/ Staff/ Getty Images, p. 4; Timothy A. Clary/ Contributor/ Getty Images, pp. 4–5; Douglas P. DeFelice/ Contributor Getty Images, pp. 6–7, 7 (Mahomes); Oasisamuel, p. 7 (Chiefs flag); Victor Texcucano/ AP Images, pp. 8, 9; Dan Thornberg, p. 9 (hobby): AlenKadr, p. 9 (food): Everett Collection, Inc./ Alamy, p. 9 (movie); Debby Wong, p. 9 (baseball player); John Weast/ Contributor/ Getty Images, p. 10; Ronald Martinez/ Staff/ Getty Images, p. 11; Chelsea Purgahn/ AP Images, p. 12; Icon Sportswire/ Contributor/ Getty Images, p. 13; Paparacy, p. 13 (Kansas City, Missouri); Jamie Squire/ Staff/ Getty Images, pp. 14–15, 18 (2018); Ben Liebenberg/ AP Images, p. 15: Kansas City Star/ Contributor Getty Images, pp. 16–17, 17; Raffaelez, p. 18 (2017); Mike Ehrmann/ Staff/ Getty Images, pp. 18–19, 23: Ryan Kang/ AP Images, p. 19 (2020); Ed Zurga/ Stringer/ Getty Images, p. 20; Don Juan Moore/ Contributor/ Getty Images, p. 21.

24